Be Fabulous

This book belongs to

- -

Fabulous in High Heels™

Fabulous in High Heels

By Sarah Toner

Illustrated by Ivana Nohel

This book is dedicated to
Sebastian, Molly and Lulu
(...to infinity and beyond).

Foreword

When I first met Sarah I was a hopeless case. Not just a yo-yo dieter but a yo-yo exerciser as well.

I jogged till my knees hurt – walked and jogged – jogged, power-walked and sprinted in sequence – or donned terrible leotards that someone had designed to make legs look longer. Wrong! People can always tell where your legs stop and that unattractive stomach/groin area begins. No eye was ever thus deceived.

I aerobic-ed to Jane Fonda, and bopped and bounced and pulled on long pieces of rubber till I was catapulted into A&E with gym whiplash. I switched on the telly every morning and watched ladies on mats in Sydney Harbour stepping and punching and lunging, and with every step and lunge they just looked sweatier and squarer. I became aware of the square aerobic body, all muscle and fitness and leotard. Those bodies that come up and say, 'Look! I've been to the gym.'

'I know, I can tell. You're square shaped.'

These women are so fit but look like Dick Emery when they put on a pair of heels. All wrong.

So I slumped into my fatness only to be rescued by the gorgeous Miss Toner. She was recommended by a friend who could see me falling into a 'I hate every kind of exercise and by the way I have bad knees and by now a very bad back' abyss. When I first met her I did not think this was a match made in heaven. She arrived all tall and slim and beautiful as ballerinas should be; I thought this is never going to work and yet, within a year, I was in point shoes. I was 'en pointe'. Something I had imagined would almost go against the laws of Nature. But Nature had not reckoned on Sarah Toner!

Sarah is a wonderful teacher and motivator and she makes it fun. She can make you laugh. She can make you laugh almost to the point of not feeling the pain (or 'the burn' as the square aerobic-ers would call it). She taught me to think about how I should move in a totally different way.

Stretching and lengthening – elegance through strength! No more spinning and wobbling on jiggling machines and pointless weights. I'm too old and, frankly, bored. I just want to have fun and feel relaxed and upright and great.

This book is about helping women feel great – read on…

Jennifer Saunders

Introduction

Whilst enjoying a brief moment in the sunshine, during a busy day of teaching ballet, I was approached by an extraordinarily beautiful man. Was this my lucky day? Are the gods really that kind?! It turned out he was a drag artist and had been admiring my walk... C'est la vie!

Female impersonators practise the art of wearing high heels usually to perfection, but what about us women? Shouldn't we also practise?

As we sat together sharing tips and observing women struggling in their heels, the answer became crystal clear... Yes, we should!

I formatted a class using tips and techniques learnt during my career as a dancer, model and dance teacher. I tested it on my new friend and he loved it! I then taught four other women how to walk in high heels: a doctor, an investment banker, a full-time mum and a writer. They enjoyed it and felt that the class did as much for their self-esteem as it did for their posture and heel-wearing technique. This was very encouraging.

I invited members of the press to participate in a class and suddenly women were coming from all over the world! The beauty, fun and laughter, as I taught these women, gave me the inspiration to write this book.

For those of you who have already taken class with me, this will be a fun reminder... and for all of you, may this book be an enjoyable experience and the beginning of a fabulous new you!

On a more serious note, please exercise carefully. If you are unsure of any exercises in this book, please ask advice from a professional fitness instructor. Seek medical advice if you are pregnant, are injured or have any condition which could prevent you from performing the exercises correctly or safely.

Sarah Toner

How the book works...

You are about to meet three 'Fabulous in High Heels' Girls. They came to Sarah Toner because they wanted to learn how to walk, look and feel great in their high heels. Who better to teach them than a ballerina? Before they embarked on the FIHH Master Class, they expected a catwalk style lesson but instead found themselves improving their posture; massaging their feet, lengthening and strengthening the muscles of their legs plus finding their 'core' stability. All this before they were even allowed anywhere near their heels!

Good posture is the key to carrying off a light and sexy walk in heels (or even without heels) and this doesn't happen without paying some attention to your body, especially your core strength.

Within these pages you will find the key exercises that Liz, Lulu and Molly learned to help them on their mission to become 'Fabulous in High Heels'. Even if you are not an avid heel wearer, you will still benefit from the exercises in this book as they will help you to attain wonderful deportment... giving you an air of supreme confidence!

Make sure you visit our website
www.fabinhighheels.com
for more ways to look and feel fabulous!

Meet the 'Fabulous in High Heels' Girls...

They are looking for help. All three have important occasions coming up…

Lulu has a high profile presentation at work which could lead to a life-changing promotion.

HERE FALLS THE BRIDE...

Molly needs some help for her wedding day...

Liz (divorced), doing a marvellous job of raising four children (on her own!)... finally has time to date the man of her dreams.

Take time to care for your feet before slipping them into your favourite heels...
and think about your posture too. Paying attention to your hair, make-up and
wardrobe is wonderful but it will all go to waste if your posture lets you down...
this includes the way you walk.

O.K, girls...

we will now begin our mission to feel and look fabulous!

These exercises are going to help you to relax, stretch and strengthen your feet. They will improve circulation and also make you aware of how intricate your feet are. Underneath the skin of each foot (soft or hard), is a beautiful network of bones, twenty-six in all. Our feet deserve to be looked after, especially by those of us who love to wear high heels.

Let's relax!

Sit on a comfy chair or stool. Cross one leg over the other, placing your ankle over the opposite knee. Firmly massage the entire sole of your foot including the heel and ball.

Take your time...

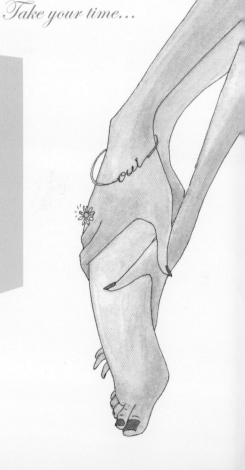

You are making your feet very happy.

Let's move on to your toes...

Still in the same position, start with your big and second toes. Part them forward and back and repeat, then part them sideways.

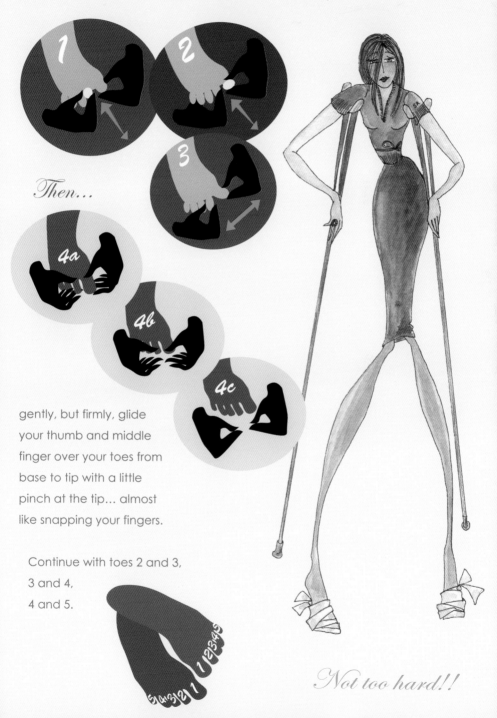

Then...

gently, but firmly, glide your thumb and middle finger over your toes from base to tip with a little pinch at the tip... almost like snapping your fingers.

Continue with toes 2 and 3,
3 and 4,
4 and 5.

Not too hard!!

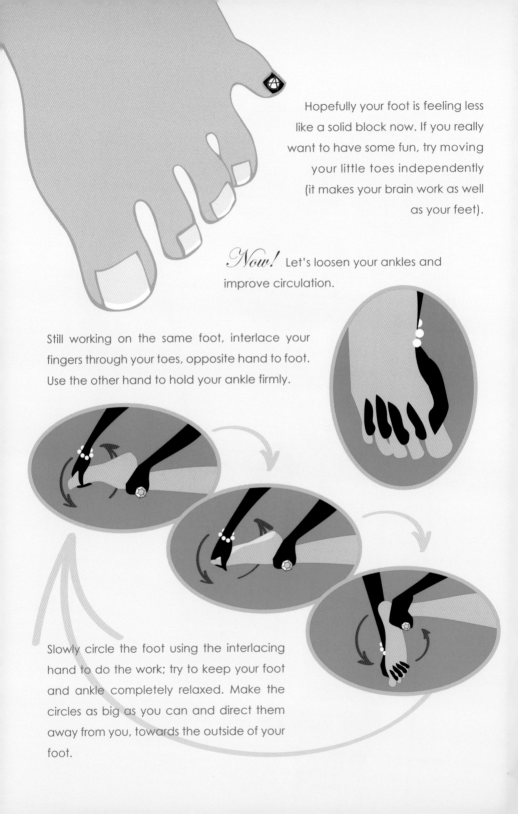

Hopefully your foot is feeling less like a solid block now. If you really want to have some fun, try moving your little toes independently (it makes your brain work as well as your feet).

Now! Let's loosen your ankles and improve circulation.

Still working on the same foot, interlace your fingers through your toes, opposite hand to foot. Use the other hand to hold your ankle firmly.

Slowly circle the foot using the interlacing hand to do the work; try to keep your foot and ankle completely relaxed. Make the circles as big as you can and direct them away from you, towards the outside of your foot.

Here's more...

Starting at your ankle as if you are wringing out a thick cloth, firmly wring your way along your foot until you reach the tips of your toes. Do this at least four times.

Repeat every exercise with the other foot and then move on to the next page. When you have finished, your feet will be feeling warm and awake.

It's time to use both feet simultaneously.

We are going to carry on improving the flexibility in your feet and ankles.
Still sitting on the chair; place both your feet flat on the floor, keep them
parallel to each other, and a few inches apart.
Lift your heels until you are completely on the tips of your toes.

Circle your feet outwards until you have brought them back to the original
position. Repeat eight times.

Repeat
8
times

Now reverse the action by circling your feet inwards.

Remain seated for just a little longer... remember to sit up tall so that you are not spreading your bottom all over the seat!

You need strength in your metatarsals and ankles to keep your feet steady in your heels. Weak, wobbly ankles look awful and are exhausting for the 'Fabulous in High Heels' girl!

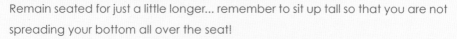

metatarsals

Try this...

Scrunch your toes and make a bridge with your feet by shunting your heels towards your toes.

Continue by raising your toes from the floor and arching them back as far as you can.

Finish by lowering the balls of the feet, with the toes still arched, then release the toes forward and try to spread them apart at the same time. Your feet will have walked forward a little.

Repeat **3** *times*

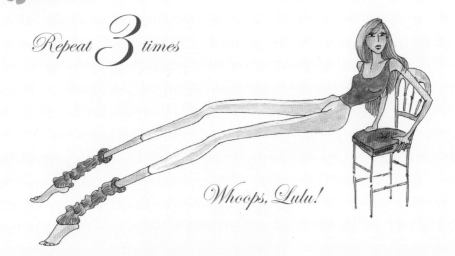

Whoops, Lulu!

Now reverse…

Scrunch your toes and make a bridge as before. This time push up onto the balls of your feet and relax your toes, then lower your heels.

Repeat **3** *times*

You should have returned to your starting position.

Careful, Molly!

Girls, it is time to stand up!

Wearing high heels can really tighten your calf muscles and you will want your heels to touch the floor when you return to your flats!

A calf stretch for you...

Hold onto the back of your chair, or put your hands against the wall, and place your feet together. Make yourself as tall as you can but without lifting your shoulders. In other words, girls, NO slouching!

Step back, keeping the leg that is stepping back straight; lower your heel to the floor, and bend your front leg. Your crotch needs to be aiming straight down to the floor. Repeat two or three times with each leg.

Take the stretch a little further, if you like, by slightly bending the back leg whilst still trying to keep the heel on the floor. No need to bend the leg too far.

Remember, during this exercise, not to let your bottom stick out or you will not reach your optimum stretch.

If you are wearing very high heels, I want your insteps to feel comfortable in this position and not overstretched. So let's try an exercise to help you strengthen and increase the arch of your foot. Those of you who have ever taken ballet classes will know this as a parallel tendu exercise. Women who haven't taken ballet, here's how it goes...

Stand sideways to your chair and hold on to it with one hand. Place the other hand on your hip and put your feet together in a parallel position.

Keeping both legs straight, slide one foot forward until your instep is as arched as it can be but the ball of your foot is still making contact with the floor. Your instep should be stretched and your legs straight, while you push to the tips of your toes (do not put any weight on your toes).

Now reverse the process; relax your toes while keeping your instep arched, then slowly slide your foot back to the original parallel position. Keep alternating feet, at least ten times.

Oh dear, Lulu...
A little too much weight on your toes!

Patience, Liz!

Just a little more work... and then you can put those gorgeous heels on!

This will strengthen your legs, ankles and feet at the same time. Try to hold your stomach in too!

Continue facing the wall or holding the back of your chair. With feet together, slowly raise your heels until you are as high as you can be on the balls of your feet. Keep your toes relaxed and your knees straight, your thighs connected and stomach held in – oh – and no bottoms sticking out.

NO! Lulu…

Like this…

Finally...

Girls, it is time to pay a little attention to your inside thighs, pelvic floor and abdomen. We need to zip it all in!

Ideally you would use a twist board for this exercise but here is a version for you until you decide whether or not to invest in one.

Hold the back of your chair or place the palms of your hands against a wall. Stand with your feet together and feel as if you are squeezing an orange between your thighs.

Somewhere between
a Satsuma and a
Jaffa, Liz!

Stand as tall as you can, without lifting your shoulders, and imagine you are lengthening your body around the area where your waist is… or perhaps 'was'!

Keep your eyes, chest and shoulders facing straight ahead and raise your heels just about one centimetre off the floor.

Now, without dropping the orange, move your heels slightly to the right but keep your shoulders level and facing forward (think Barbie... those dolls swivel at the waist!). Return to your starting position and then move your heels to the left.

Repeat this swivel for as long as you like; remembering to squeeze the orange, lengthen your waist and keep your shoulders down and facing forward.

Oh… and stomachs in at all times.
Which leads me to…

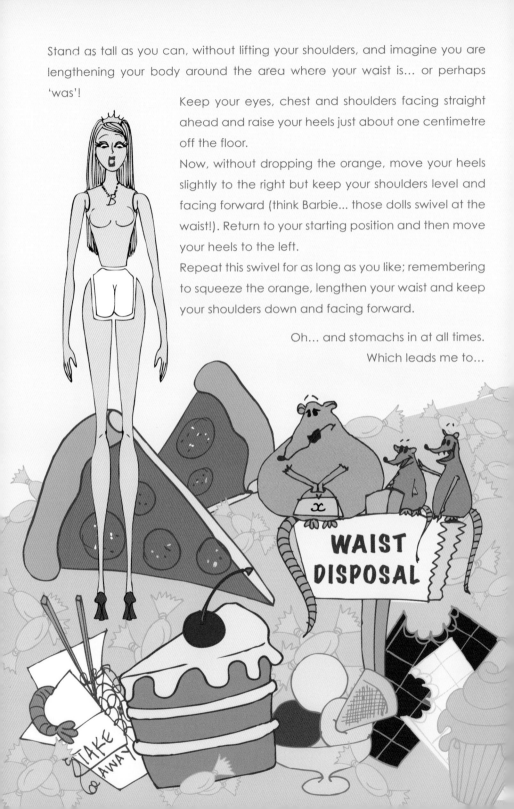

WAIST DISPOSAL

TAKE AWAY

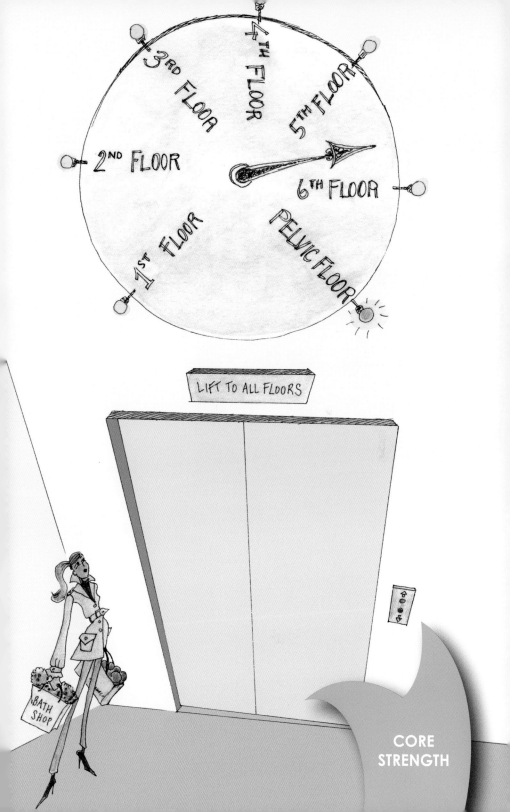

This...

I know you are desperate to get your shoes on, and I know I said we were performing our final exercise, but there is just one other very helpful thing that I would love to share with you... particularly those of you who have children. You REALLY need to use your imagination for this one!

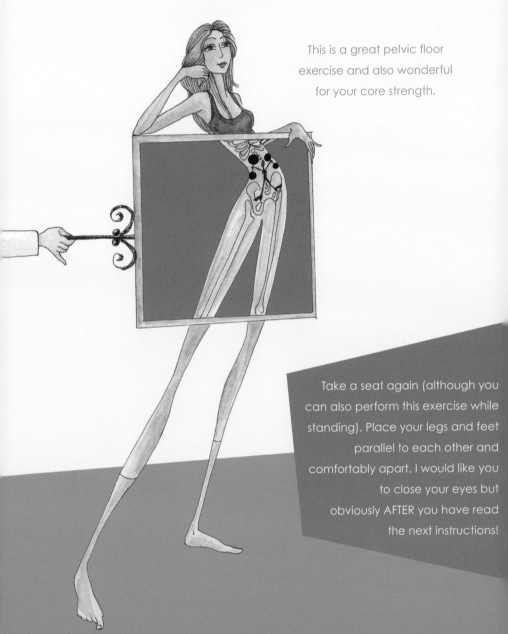

This is a great pelvic floor exercise and also wonderful for your core strength.

Take a seat again (although you can also perform this exercise while standing). Place your legs and feet parallel to each other and comfortably apart. I would like you to close your eyes but obviously AFTER you have read the next instructions!

Picture this: in your abdomen you have a football-shaped sponge, a number 3 or 4 ball for anybody who has a son or two or who knows footballs. Imagine the sponge is full of water.

I want you to squeeze all the water out of the sponge BUT it must keep its spherical shape. In other words, you need to find muscles to squeeze all surface areas of the ball.

At the same time, you must not let any of the water escape.

Hold this for as long as you can remembering, as always, to keep your back straight. Do NOT worry if you can't feel the correct sensation immediately (you will eventually!).

Repeat as many times as you can, or until you realise that you will be late for your date, appointment or wedding!

So close your eyes, squeeze hard, and return to the book when you are done. By the way, after all that squeezing, you may need a bathroom break!

Now now, up you get!

Pour your beautifully relaxed and
strengthened feet into your shoes
and let's get really fabulous!

We will work from the shoes up!

Take a look at your feet.
Now take a look at the time:
12.55 on the clock.
NO! Not a digital clock.

Place your feet just inside the time five to one. Your heels will be together and your big toes roughly an inch apart. Make sure that you have rotated the legs as well as the feet to achieve this position.

Try a couple of circuits of your room with your feet in this position. As you walk with your legs and feet turned slightly out, you will feel stronger and more centred in your hips. If you walk towards a mirror, I think you will like what you see... a more flattering angle of your feet... and shoes.

Next we need to release some tension from your knees.

Once more, return to the chair, sit down and lift your thigh off the seat.
Take the full weight of your thigh by cradling it in your hands. Now
swing your lower leg forward and back, like a pendulum, using NO

muscles – let it swing freely. Repeat with the other leg, and
then continue by alternating legs. This exercise is easy and
relaxing so keep swinging for as long as you like.

LIBERATE YOUR KNEES!

Take another walk whilst recalling the lovely liberated
sensation in your knees. You may notice the
beginnings of a gentle lilt in your hips... wonderful!

It's time to apply all that wonderful work you did to your core.

Take 3 seconds to recall the orange, and of course the sponge!

Take another walk and feel the strength and control in your core. This will complete the strong yet relaxed lilt to your walk that began with your 'free from tension' knees.

There's more...

Come on, we're nearly there! Have a think about your arms. Do you swing them as if you are marching? Are they rigid? Are you permanently holding a handbag that isn't there?

Try this simple exercise to get a relaxed and beautiful swing to your arms.
As you walk around the room pat the thigh of the leg that you are stepping forward onto with the opposite hand.

Keep this up for a few minutes or until you have sorted out your coordination.

When you are ready, stop patting your thighs but keep your arms swinging slightly and gently across your body, making sure that your elbows are relaxed.
Feel like a model? Good! But in fact your posture will be better than a model's.

Take a seat again, girls. Let's release some tension in our shoulders and improve the posture in our upper backs at the same time.

Sit up beautifully straight, with your sponge in place, of course. Now, without any rounding or pushing back of your shoulders, raise them as high as you can. Still with your shoulders lifted, take a deep breath in and at the same time rotate your arms so that the palms of your hands are facing forwards and the fingertips are pointing straight down to the floor. Slowly exhale, keep your arms rotated, lower your shoulders by concentrating on the muscles across your upper and middle back, and pull down towards the floor with your fingertips. If you sit sideways to a mirror and take a peek afterwards you may be pleasantly surprised at the change in your posture.

Oh dear, Lulu...

Try walking again, paying attention to the new, improved posture in your back. Enjoy your gentle arm swing, and the fact that you will be walking taller than ever before!

To ensure that your neck is relaxed and to prevent you from poking your chin forward, or dropping it down in the double chin look...

Take hold of the very tips of your ears, the backs of your hands should be facing upwards, and your fingertips pointing straight down.
Relax your neck, pull your ears very gently towards the ceiling and feel the wonderful release of tension in the neck, head and face.

You can put a small amount of pressure on the side of the head to prevent your ears from becoming sore. You should feel as if you have made a little space between each vertebra. Make a GENTLE 'NO' movement with the head, just to check you have really found freedom.

A final tip...

Keep your eyes off the floor; try to fix on a point several metres away when you are walking rather than down at your feet. Looking down will round your shoulders and strain your neck, plus you will not look or feel confident, or fabulous!

Here is my ultimate
'Fabulous in High Heels'
gift to you, girls...

DO NOT RUSH

Nothing looks more sexy and confident than a
woman who is taking her time. The world is a busy
place and to glide through it in a slow and relaxed
manner might just give you that
'Je ne sais quoi...' you have always desired!

So that's it!

If you have followed these exercises you have worked hard. Hopefully you are feeling more comfortable and confident in your body, your shoes and maybe in your mind too.

You are ready for your final lap of honour.

Congratulations!

Pat yourself on the back.... or each other, if you are with a friend.

Say, "I look Fabulous in High Heels!"

Grab your coats, your handbags, your best friend or partner, and hit the town with the knowledge that you look...

Fabulous in high heels!

So how did the 'Fabulous in High Heels' girls get on?
Lulu was promoted.

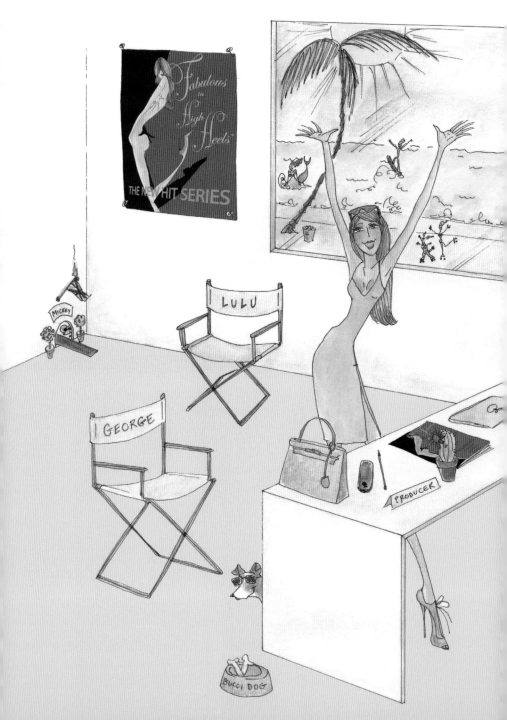

Molly was the most fabulously elegant
bride they had ever seen...

Liz's date?

The End

The Beginning...
of a fabulous new you.

Liz's Wish List

A beautiful, happy home

*C*ycle across Europe on a NEW bicycle

*T*o give my parents every comfort

*T*o dance on stage again

*T*o sing backing vocals for Van Morrison

*T*o write the lyrics for a string of hit songs

A pair of sparkling (but 'ethical') diamond earrings

*T*o see my daughters grow up happy and fulfilled

*T*o see a total eclipse

Molly's Wish List

*T*o be a main character in a film

*T*o have 4 children: 2 girls and 2 boys

*T*o find a cure for AIDS

*T*o travel to as many countries
and to see as many of the wonders
of the world as I possibly can

*T*o live in America

*T*o have saxophone lessons

... and then to play in a band

*R*ide a horse at a gallop!

*T*ry being a blonde!

*T*o find life in space

Lulu's Wish List

Own the largest collection of shoes in the world

Change careers and become a vet

Take a cookery course

Design a T-shirt for breast cancer

Surprise my best friend with the holiday of a lifetime

Go on a date with George Clooney

Learn how to fly ... (not literally!!)

Foster children

Own a pink Corvette

Sing in a choir

Fabulous in High Heels

My Wish List

all wishes are drawn in these bubbles

May your bubbles never burst

Acknowledgements

with love, from Sarah

The appreciative audiences whom I have performed for

The fabulous and inspirational dancers and teachers throughout my training and career

The dedicated students & clients I have had the joy to teach

Jennifer

Liz

Ivana

My Dad

Dan

L + S + M = ♥

About us..

When my lovely (but very naughty) Jack Russell terrier first met Ivana, he didn't know whether to run away, attack or submit. He ended up doing all three. I must admit, I completely understand where he was coming from! But Ivana is far too intriguing and enticing to run away from, and she knows it. She has the strongest sense of self you are likely to meet and she stands patiently and confidently until you have figured that out... then she watches while you rise to her (very) high expectations. Ivana is phenomenally talented. In her life and work everything is possible and there is never time for self-indulgent negativity. 'Good' is not good enough, 'great' is 'ok'..."fabulous / fantastic / brilliant" let you know that you might be on the right track when you are working with her!' Mediocre is likely to make Ivana gag involuntarily so don't even go there! She is a role model extraordinaire, for women and men everywhere. Oh! And dogs too!!

Before I met Sarah, she existed in my fairy tales. Upon meeting her, my instinct was too offer her a shiny, RED ...mmmm ... delicious... apple! Alas, and fortunately for me, she enchanted me. Graceful, gentle, kind, generous, intelligent, creative and a thoroughly captivating storyteller, in my (eagle) eyes, Sarah is gift to all of the lives she touches. Sarah is a woman from another, more beautiful universe; Dancer, Writer, Artist and VERY yummy Mummy! ...so full of joy, energy, humour, zest and optimism despite any obstacles that life throws in her path. Yes ladies, it seems everyone has obstacles, despite the length of their legs!

Sarah Toner photo: www.nickdelaney.com   Ivana Nohel photo: Charles Fegen

Q. Who is this much loved celebrity? Here are a few clues...

Award winning actress, comedian and writer. One half of the funniest comedy duo ever. Hit, after hit, after hit, television series...

A. It's the one and only, the beautiful, the incredible... Jennifer Saunders!